DOUBLES

Phoenix Poets

A SERIES EDITED BY ALAN SHAPIRO

DOUBLES

ROBERT POLITO

THE UNIVERSITY OF CHICAGO PRESS
Chicago and London

Robert Polito is director of the Writing Program at the New School for Social Research, New York. He is the author of *Savage Art: A Biography of Jim Thompson* and *A Reader's Guide to James Merrill's The Changing Light at Sandover.*

The University of Chicago Press, Chicago 60637
The University of Chicago Press, Ltd., London
© 1995 by The University of Chicago
All rights reserved. Published 1995
Printed in the United States of America

04 03 02 01 00 99 98 97 96 95   1 2 3 4 5

ISBN 0–226–67337–5 (cloth)
       0–226–67338–3 (paper)

Library of Congress Cataloging-in-Publication Data

Polito, Robert
        Doubles / Robert Polito.
            p. cm. — (Phoenix poets)
        I. Title. II. Series.
        PS3566.0474D68 1995
        813'.54—dc20   95-2818
                                                              CIP

Contents

Acknowledgments

The author gratefully acknowledges the editors and publishers of the following publications, in which these poems first appeared:

AGNI: "Animal Mimicry," "Doubles"
Chelsea: "Not the Right Way"
The New Yorker: "What the Dead Know"
Pequod: "Evidence"
Ploughshares: "Cathy's Braces"(13, no. 4), "Cigarette Lighter" (9, no. 1), "First Love" (9, no. 1), "Those Fireflies, for Instance" (5, no. 2),"To My Father" (17, nos. 2 and 3)
Yale Review: "Nana"

"Evidence" also appeared in *Best American Poetry, 1991,* edited by Mark Strand and David Lehman; "Animal Mimicry" also appeared in *Walk on the Wild Side: American Urban Poetry Since 1975,* edited by Nicholas Christopher; and "First Love" also appeared in *The Ploughshares Poetry Reader,* edited by Joyce Peseroff.

"Animal Mimicry" draws on an essay, "Mimicry and Legendary Psychasthenia," by Roger Caillois, translated by John Shepley (*October,* no. 28, 1984).

DOUBLES

Animal Mimicry

The sun's setting in another part of the city.
Backlit by a pink bulb slung from an orange cord
Topless Dallas shimmies to her full six feet, palms

Her breasts and gazes into deep space
Before catching her captive audience. Shivering
Once she laughs across the airless airshaft—

"Looks like you're all moved in. Love
The new plants! Lots of, huh, privacy . . ."

Drawing the petalled curtains. Back to
The keyboard—her novel; we unpack more cartons.
Her spaniel's low moan inhabits our bedroom every midnight.

•

Life takes a step forward
Or back.

Box crabs resemble rounded pebbles;
Rocks recall brains.

Beetles identical with rose petals
Adorn a rose bush.

The spots of the Kallima simulate lichens—lichens
Streaked with the knots of the poplars they grow on.

The *Cilax compressa* is confused
With bird droppings.

·

Five weeks here and I move like a native,
A brisk grinding tread that's a Hobson's Choice
Between jail break and death march;

Rearending a tourist stalled with his bags
By the intersection of Walk
& Don't Walk, I pitch my body against the traffic—

As if cars and I were equal;
As if all we could do is kill.

Eyes trained on an inner horizon
(But taking everything in, giving nothing back)
I look up into the mirrored

Doorway of the Love Pharmacy to discover
A junkie hawking birdcages—
And myself in a crow-black suit

Chattering to myself. Instinctively
I sense I'm home.

·

As a boy snorkeling off Bimini with my Dad

I saw, I swear, black through the sapphire water
An octopus retract its tentacles, curve
Its back, adapt its color, and sink to the floor

A stone . . . Like his cock and balls at the chilly Y
Pool, when we swam nude, withdrawn
To a fluted snail and shell—

No bigger than my own, I shouted,

Until I looked down. Years later in the cancer ward
He asked me to hold him up

While he dripped blood
Into a blue plastic cup.

          •

Nights we commune with our fat cat
Elvis, black genius of the new

And old house, his cool ruffled
By sirens, backfirings, screams,

As sightings of the abdicated self-
Exiled sovereign whose name

He bears awaken K-Marts
In Athens and Memphis.

The Chinese, I console him,
Transliterate Elvis

"The King of Cats"—
But still his nerves rasp;

Sleepless, as ten flights down
Another semi shatters Amsterdam,

He mimes a stoic stretch and yawn
(Others he saved,

Himself he could not save)
The next best thing to not being there.

       •

Geometer-moths so match shoots of shrubbery
Gardeners cut them with pruning shears;

Phillia browse among themselves,
Taking each other for real leaves.

Startled creatures.

The instinct for self-preservation playing
Leapfrog

With the instinct for renunciation.

       •

From a late dinner at the Marlin we return loaded
To face a short, swaying man and a doberman he calls My Gun;

Mica in the concrete sets stars winking along the sidewalk,
His acne scars repeat the coarse brick of our building;

A look that translates, it's only money, babes,
And My Gun talking for him at our feet,
I make a show of emptying my wallet;

Yeah, the plastic, he barks, and her purse,
Your watch . . . Those wedding rings,
Keep 'em; I say they always bad luck . . .

Canines grinding, nose high, rearing
On his chain, sniffing,
Gnarling—

Down boy, what you trying to say?
Smart Baby! I think My Gun wants I
Investigate your pockets . . .

You sly dog you, he grins at
Me, while sheepishly I hand over
Twenty-four more dollars.

Look at it like this way,
You buying time;
Place to live—

Till ya meet up with My Gun
Again.

Now might we walk you
To your door?

I-guess-you'd-say,
What-can-make-me-feel-this-way?

My Gun, talking 'bout My Gun . . .

You all have nice night.

We see you around.

Doubles

I fancy myself an enigma.
            On my best days
I manage to keep the world off-guard—
            What I say
Does not follow from what I said yesterday.
            Or the message in my clothes
Is somehow inconsistent with my face—
            A banker's striped suit
Under shades and a flashy pompadour.

            Around me
People must continually readjust;
            I force them
Always to approach me on my own terms—
            Only I keep
Changing those terms, keep shifting ground.
            Around me
The angle of incidence does *not* equal
            The angle of reflection.

It's not that I have any secrets,
        Or a secret life;
If anything, my life's what's left in the shell
        After the clam's been eaten—
So I arrange to have many lives, many stories,
        All of them plausible
—Taken one by one—but not quite adding up.
        It's a lot of work,
Yet the looks I get, the odd questions I'm asked,

        Would repay any trouble . . .
Sometimes when I'm very tired I think
        How nice it must be
Just to trot out this year's model and keep him there.
        But then I remember
What I've gained: to be all men at once,
        Without being anyone—
And I recall the danger too: staying put is like *asking*
        The world to do you in.

But these aren't real issues anymore.
        All problems stopped
Right after my order was delivered from the Institute,
        Two huge bundles
Wrapped tight in black paper and cold to touch—
        My contact had insisted
"One to a customer," but I cheated a bit,
        Claimed I was twins,
Identical twins, so he sent a pair.

Unpacked, released
From their tubs of dry ice, even as they stood
Frozen and immobile
I could see they were marvels: whole, self-
Sustaining universes
Of cells spun from two of mine, my equals down to
The last hair and birthmark;
And thawed, breathing freely, they lacked only a history.
Such details

Are absorbed more easily than you'd think:
Like me, they're fast
Studies; hardly a week of pleasantly intense
Afternoons goes by,
And provided with the necessary names,
A few photographs,
Some not entirely congruent "facts," and the basic
Rules of presentation,
They seem more emphatically me than I've ever felt.

I have great plans for us—
One I'm coaching so that soon
He'll be a star;
Every night in clubs he gets applause for singing *my* songs:
"When the smack
Begins to flow then I really don't care anymore."
Or "Every time I phone you
I just want to put you down"—exhilarating words,
So angry and bitter

I'd be afraid to say them in real life.
                    The other's
Just received his second promotion at the bank,
                    And there's talk
He'll be a vice president before he's forty . . .
                    But I don't have to do anything.
I can read all night, listen to records, or drink,
                    Without worrying
Whether I'll be able to go to work in the morning.

                    It doesn't matter
If I get up, or what I eat, or how I look—
                    I'm completely free.
No matter what I do, my life goes on without me!
                    Sometimes in disguise
I visit them—to check up or keep in touch—
                    And request a song, or a loan.
They usually indulge me. Has any father
                    Ever been this proud?

And always I'm amazed at how effortlessly they handle
                    All that I've found impossible—
Through long distracting lunches with my mother
                    They smile and hold their tempers;
They remember birthdays, keep appointments, pay bills;
                    I'm never feeling well,
But they're healthy—moderate habits, exercise, periodic
                    Trips to a doctor.
In their hands, my life positively hums.

Yes, things are looking up.
I sense that everyone is talking about us.
Word's come back to me
That the inevitable double sighting has taken place . . .
Imagine trying to explain that.
And in the paper I see that one of us has broken
Off an engagement—
That's the spirit! She's not good enough,
Hold out for bigger stakes!

I joke—what could make me happier?
One of us
Must settle down soon and start a family;
What we have
Is too rich, too perfect just to pass away.
But I want the last
Word here too: when I die, I've asked them to bury me
Quietly, anonymously,
And go on as if nothing's happened.

Not the Right Way

Why did God make me this way?
"Brain damaged"; but not so much that I don't know it.
I can't seem to do anything the right way.

I keep finding this out every day.
I make mistakes. Everyone tells me it
Would be different if God hadn't made me this way.

Once I heard my mother say
Something in my head died because no air reached it.
Is that why I can't do anything the right way?

I don't understand why I make people angry.
Sometimes they laugh at me. I don't think they can help it.
Is it just that God made me this way?

When I can't sleep, I pray
God, whatever you did to me, please undo it.
I want to do things the right way.

When my mother dies, I'll move far away
And I won't speak to anyone again. It's
Worse when I talk—but why did God make me this way?
Always the same, and not the right way.

Nana

Sunday evening, the downtown shut up;
Above the arcade of stores and stands, blazing over-
Time, sodium vapor lamps pick out

A few hand-holding couples, in from
The suburbs, or drifted down from the Public Gardens,
Busily checking their reflections in display windows

Whose fierce mannequins, hands on
Hips, and this year proud as prize Japanese carp
In spotted kimonos, trailing silks, and fans,

Tilt back their necks to mock
Her HEAVY METAL T-shirt and ironed jeans, his drooping
Belly and gold chains—

On my way to drinks and dinner in the North End
I duck past Arch Street Chapel
And almost knock down an old woman.

Steadying her, recovering her squat purse,
Leather missal and splayed holy cards
—Her salvation, her many dead, face up on the sidewalk;

Mrs. Kearney? (My grandmother's oldest crony,
In her nineties and still, according to my mother, battling
The local toughs who heave beer cans on her lawn.)

No—. Airy veil hairpinned to her curls,
In a long dress dense with lilacs, thick flesh-colored stockings,
Rosary wound twice around her left wrist,

She could be Nana, not dead these
17 years,
But walking away from her second Mass of the day.

When grabbing after the tail of the senile
Mongrel I sensed you loved only
A little less than me,

I skidded into a sideboard
And sent an antique lazy Susan whirling
Into splinters,

It was you who sought the blame—
Met my parents' disbelieving stares
With a jumbled, bold-faced tale about "dusting," "a dizzy spell,"

And didn't flinch;
And when Butch began snapping back at me,
You had him destroyed.

Afternoons, alone in the dark flat,
You made butter and sugar sandwiches; from newspaper
Unfolded boats and hats;

Taught me to trace, and—for purposes utterly
Up your dark sleeves—how to assemble a coffee pot;
Later, we crossed the boulevard at the end of the street.

The world you promised
Appeared to fashion itself largely from clothes—
When I won a small scholarship to high school

You laughed and clapped your hands,
Percolated that now I could buy suits, sweaters,
"Everything you'll ever want!"

Manners, too. That last morning
On the way to the hospital,   .
Knowing I wouldn't be allowed to visit

—You were about to die, who didn't say so?—
You dragged and wheezed up the stairs to my room.
. . . Which means, I should have told this old woman

I'm sorry.
—Yet she's already halfway down the block.
I start to chase after her, carefully, shouting ahead

So that my leather jacket and noisy boots won't spook her;
Until she spins,
Beads and cross swinging, fist reaching up into the lights:

"Stay away from me! Damn you! If you'd see where you're going
You wouldn't need to say you're sorry—
Goddamn stupid kid."

First Love

The day's too beautiful;
The spring sun on the porch too warm . . .
He's restless; nothing can contain him—
Not his books, or a whole house full of toys,
Not even the hidden fortress he's built
Deep in his grandmother's garden—

For this is his special day.
His secret love is coming to have dinner
With his parents, *with him*—
Irish, plump, black hair
Set like a helmet over her red face;
An old student of his mother's dead sister,
Smelling of soap and flowers,
He can't wait to see what she's brought him,
Can't wait for her soft words, her wet kiss . . .

So he decides to meet her car.
First, he skips to the corner of the street,
And waits . . . A half hour seems to go by
But still no sign of her great black Chrysler;
He thinks he knows her route,
Recalling the day she drove them to her house,
And slowly he sets off, one street at a time,
Stopping at each new corner to look all around—
Down the street they take to Mass,

With its wall of trim, brown three-deckers;
Along a wide avenue, divided by a strip of land
Where there are benches and trees;
Then he's not so sure where he is anymore—
Suddenly there's what looks like a highway;
So he starts walking in the other direction,
Trying to retrace his steps,
But it's all new to him, unfamiliar.
He keeps on walking until he's too tired to go on,
And humiliated, lonely,
He sits down on another porch, and begins to cry.

He's certain he'll never see his parents again,
Never see Barbara,
When a minister he mistakes for a priest
Comes out of his house, and saves him.
He brings him inside, asks his name,
And goes to the phone;
Returning, he says, "They sound like nice people.
You know they've been very worried about you."

The minister's wife, and their two grown daughters,
Make much of him—they sit him in the sun,
Stop his crying, wash his face,
And feed him soda and cake.
He can't remember ever being treated so nice—
He feels like the young prince in one of his storybooks.

But at last there's her black car—
Once again in tears, he runs to them,
To Barbara, to his mother and father,
Telling them over and over
That he didn't run away, that he loves them,
That all he wanted to do was *meet her car*—

His mother's crying, and Barbara,
They hug him, and say they're glad to have him back . . .
His father too—

                But suddenly *he* seems confused;
He pulls his son away from the two women,
And starts to shake him—

                    "Do you understand
How much trouble you've caused us?
Do you know that you walked *over five miles?*
That's one for every year of your life"—

He seems about to hit him;
Anger and awe alternate on his face—

                        Just like the time
The boy received his first toolbox,
And went off by himself for an entire afternoon,
And patiently, methodically,
Sawed the railing off the back porch—
His father furious,
But amazed that he could do that with a toy saw—

Anger and awe crisscrossing his face,
Like crosshatching,
Or like those cheap prints
Where the rabbit becomes a duck,
And the beautiful girl turns into a skull grinning from ear to ear;

His awe equal to his anger—
So that, in the end, he's unable to strike.

To My Father

Father, this night
As on so many other nights
I envy you.

Not as an infatuated child
Is jealous of his father—
When I was a child
I desired your strength;
What I saw as your intelligence;
A thousand small skills
That I have never made my own—

I try to imagine
The disintegration of your body:
In the grave I refuse to visit
(One time twisting the steering wheel
From my mother's hands
As she tried to drive into the cemetery)
The smile Keohane's Funeral Home
Fashioned for you out of paraffin
Probably has dropped away in a piece,
A rotting strip of happiness;
The dowager's rosy pancake
Now brown, mottled, full of holes;
The great head overspread with hair
Black-and-white, still growing—

Yet I can't do it,
Can't go on.

Instead
I feel only that something is missing,
Never to turn up at the Lost and Found;
That I might dig down deep into the earth
Until all of *my* strength were gone,
And not reach you;

And that the peace death
Brought you
Is entirely the absence of struggle—

Cancer smothered you thirty days
After you woke one morning with an "upset stomach";
But you died that sunny autumn afternoon
Your doctor revealed the tumor in your liver:
I know. I was with you.
I saw you surrender and give up on your life.

Or did it end years before this?
I know from your sister
That when you returned from the Service
And lived with her and her husband
—You would have been my age now—
You supported yourself
In some vague way no one can quite remember,
Though I think you told me once
That you sold cigars through the mail;
She says that you'd stay up late every night
Reading books—five or six a week—
And filling notebooks with writing
Which either has disappeared
Or was destroyed;

And that suddenly one day you stopped.

You found a job with the Post Office;
Met and married my mother;
Took—I sense—to family life
The way other men
Turn to alcohol or gambling;
Had me; then my sister and brother . . .
You found pleasure in being a "good father."

Some nights I even envy you for that.

Not until I was in high school
And visited my friends and their parents
Did the absence of books from our home
Seem at all curious;
I asked you, and you told me
That you stopped reading
When books became "too filthy."
That seems to have been about 1950—
I would notice as the years went by
There was little before that you didn't know.
You did crossword puzzles far into the night;
You ground your teeth in your sleep
Until they had to be capped;

I was born in 1951;
You wanted me to be an engineer
And destroyed novels and records
You could not approve of—
I'm certain that no one else
Has ever doubted that you were a good father.

Father, tonight I envy you. You lost,
I think, but it's over.

Cigarette Lighter

"But it's only a cigarette lighter . . ."
—Offering
From the guarded hand of a twelve-year-old
Whose father is unable to start the briquets.
Oppressive July, the first of two weeks at the lake.
Whoosh! The flames leap up as the family scatters.

"If you have a cigarette lighter
I've got to believe that you're smoking."
Where there's fire there's . . .
That he wasn't is exactly his fervid point:
To *seem* bad, afraid really to be bad—
Zippos without smokes; tight
Iridescent suits with a green cloth bookbag
. . . James Dean as Teacher's Pet.

"I think that you better hand it over."
The chicken sizzles, spits, blackens
As father and son circle the grill.
Eyes narrow; ignite
Burning questions . . . anger, tears,
That would flare to this day

But suddenly dinner's ready;
Or . . . the boy takes aim
And the lighter, still lit,
Takes off in a long arc
Fire catching fire
Straight for the sun it gets lost in—
A hiss, or a splash,
The only sure sign that it ever comes down.

Cathy's Braces

Only seem to be there when you look for them
At first, almost a secret, except for a tiny spring

Or needle's point that peeks out from behind
What it's supposed to prop up—

Or keep back; but these silver snow fences,
Once you've located one,

The bands and wires are suddenly everywhere,
Tensed, unyielding, their presence all too visibly

Extended to hold everything inside,
Going all out to give nothing away

While they steel a ruined landscape
Against more ruin,

Running in place past
Caverns hard winds might have hollowed,

Ice filling dull, unreflecting pools,
Two trees growing away from each other . . .

The whole scene's locked up in their embrace—no eluding that.
And these fences can be taken down and packed away

Only after you can't find them anymore, their differences made,
The workers disappearing into their work,

Having seen to everything, themselves at last unseen,
In a promised Spring; but not promising, not smiling.

II

But braced against what?
I keep having to ask—

Pretty; clever;
At thirty-five looks seven, ten years younger—

Yet this:
"I couldn't find a dentist who would do it before,

They all thought my overbite was cute . . .
They forget that it's not cute as your face gets older."

It shouldn't be men,
Not with so many boyfriends, so many people chasing her—

"It's the first thing I thought about,
I would have to give up putting penises in my mouth

For two-and-a-half years. I'd rip them to pieces.
. . . You mean you didn't feel my wires? Really?"

And she can't have had them installed
For me . . . We'd only just met—

Their taut lines already drawn,
The binding rigged and springing

Into action, flexed, tightening—
"You see how I feel about you. I like you.

I love you. And you know I like
Going to bed with you—

But you're too much like him, my ex-
Husband. You wouldn't be strong enough

For me. When I'd get too intense,
Or we'd get too close, you'd be scared, you'd draw back

—Just like he did. It's a gut feeling I have.
If it weren't for that it would be a piece of cake, believe me.

I warned you about that right from the beginning,
So don't punish me now.

And I told you about this guy I used to go out with,
He wants to start seeing me again—

We didn't learn to trust each other then,
But we have to start sometime, don't we?

You'll see. You'll *thank* me. I'd drive you crazy.
So can't you just understand? I mean, *can't* you?"

Those Fireflies, for Instance

Glasses drained,
Cigars smoked to their bands,
Conversation. Deep looks. Smiles.

Night lurches, repeats itself,
Sees double in our little
Glassed-in terrace garden.
Winds down, as fog calms the city
Spun from the blue smoke
Running circles around us.

Spindles lost in foliage
Direct cooling airs—
Stately, bright, insouciant—
Conditioned as we are
To the little garden's variety.
From a corner palms,
Pushed by fans, applaud
Every deft remark,
Each winning gesture.

Who now can recall
What led us here?

The friends meet in a city square
At midday. Dazed, stunned,
Faces flushed as if drunk on the heat
Vinelike and viscous about them.
Intoxication sometimes is accompanied
By a certain clarification of vision.
Never has the city seemed so bright.
Everything is just as it appears,
Only larger, as if magnified
Like emotions in poems
Or when, in the dark, curtains fold
To reveal the intense white screen.

The city at midday is a city
Made of glass, under glass,
Fired on all sides, molten, running.
Blinded, staggering as on hot sand,

Arm-in-arm they see each other home.

Close one eye and think:
Those fireflies, for instance,
Winking at us as they luxuriate
In the leaves of our tiny elastic ash,

Their cool light calls back bright day

As happily as they reflect the constellations
Turning beyond the blue dome, motionless, above us.

What the Dead Know

Air here is like the water
Of an aquarium that's been lived in for a while—clear and still
Beyond the rigors
Of glass; appearing cold (and clear) as spring streams
Fed by snow and ice,
But unexpectedly warm to feel, and inviting; side-lit—
A vitality of shadows
Once you come into it, and long bars of light
Burning like spots,
Remarkable for the absence of dust in their sharp crossfires;
Heavy, as crystal
Is heavy, as if to move here would mean pushing against a force
Palpable, and strong;
Yet rich with prospects of life, comfortable
With the idea of life,
As if, put on its slide, every drop is stocked with wonders,
Swarming, about to burst—

Beautiful in a way,
One element sustaining another, our message brought home
So that the living
Might come to see. Harder to say that without them
We are nothing—
Water without air; or to speak of our isolation,
Or our special loneliness;
Or say as they look right through us, at their plants,
Pictures, books,
Windows, reflections, and blank white walls,
That we need them,
To orient ourselves and to tell us who we are;
Or that with each look
They are swimming to within our sights; or that we are always casting
Wider and wider
And that even now they are fighting to avoid our nets.

Evidence

> *It was one of those spots you get in. If I said some more*
> *about "personal" I would be making a mystery of it, and that's bad.*
> —Double Indemnity

1.

> *The blood-red drapes were there,*
> *but they didn't mean anything.*

On our first full night together
—Fought for; ecstatic—

Riding on desire like a drug,
Too frightened, too thrilled, to let go,

Although undone by the night,
Drained, empty, coveting sleep like a drug,

I kept driving on, never to sleep,
So that, sometime in the night, I might watch you sleep—

But I must have dozed off—
Because I came to dreaming

I was in my own bed, alone,
Flames chewing the walls of my room.

—Lord Byron, on his "treacle-moon,"
Roused by firelight through the crimson curtain
Of a four-poster, determined:
"I was fairly in hell, with Prosperine lying beside me—"

But hell, here . . . in our hotel, on West 44th Street?
I roll over to wake you; then stop—

Through the greasy, polyester drapes, the color
Of movie-blood,

Bare bulbs in the airshaft glow
Like a plug-in, portable fire from Sears . . .

—Hell, I told myself, is outside;
And starts tomorrow.

On my way to kiss your hand,
You stir, raise up, look past me,

Groan once—
Then drift off again.

"Winter, and I feel the circles of my world
Contract . . . Soon it's boots and leg-warmers—
Do you care if I become taller than you?
I guess horizontal it doesn't matter."

•

"I want to break out of all the rules, not just
The ones everybody does. There's nothing interesting
About infidelity—let's go way beyond that!"

•

"He makes me laugh by telling jokes
Or doing 'funny' things on purpose . . .
I feel I make him laugh mostly not on purpose.
Sometimes it seems confusing—"

•

"What got you interested? It's partly a question of *why me* . . .
Don't worry, though, I'm too curious to skip this one—
Hold on tight it's faster than the speed of light!"

•

"I listen to basketball games on the radio
In the car—you love Frank Sinatra;
It could be amazing . . .
But why am I doing this? I love my husband."

He was a big blocky man, about my
size, with glasses, and I played him exactly
the way I figured to.

—July. Noon. Lunch. Sun
Like a slap to the back of the neck.
Heat in visible coils above the street;
Mirage shaded in the fine brown dust
Of an adjacent construction site
A tin umbrella tensely unfold-
Ing over this sidewalk table
Or the beers I've ordered
Won't shield us from,
As the Rival collapses into his seat—
My friend; her husband;
Earnest, affable, if a little
Slow   *no*
porcine   vacant   swelling
over mugs & napkins   balloon i'm twitching
to pop   what do i what does she
see

Looking around: Next to us, frowning
Over folders, broadsides, infinite Xeroxes,
Stopping to count each new line on his fingers
A red-eyed poet shakily fills
In the squares of a notebook stamped RECORD;

A young woman in a pink sundress
Raises the *Globe* against the light:
Nominee and also-rans compete
On page one with the Jacksons' "Victory" tour
And RADIOACTIVE MAN LOOSE IN CITY.

Fiercely I keep my Ray-Bans
Plastered to my face;
So that what I don't hear myself saying
Won't burn through—
you think i'm kidding   you think   i'm crazy
i got a bomb strapped to my crotch   hear the
ticking   everybody
here   just bought a one way ticket   Sirens cut the air—

A waterglass pitches over as workers return to their machines.
No other evident signs of alarm.

4.

"... We've got to be brazen!
That day, way back, when I wore the blue skirt,
I was guessing you'd approve of something 'stylish'—
I wasn't thinking about *legs*."

•

"This might have to stop
If we decide to have a baby—
Or perhaps I'll just take my chances . . .
Thanks for being so lovely this weekend."

•

"You and I need to live in the real world;
I get afraid that you are looking for fantasies,
That the actual stuff won't be enough . . . if I think of this going on
It's got to fit some life of ours, it can't *be* our life."

•

"But I keep getting images of smashing up,
Body to body, explosions in the night, flames engulf
The house . . . I always have a tremor—
Should I try to keep a bit more distance?"

•

"Could you destroy my letters?
I'd feel better and freer about writing—
I don't want you to be hit by a truck
And. . . ."

5.

LAST TIMES: NOON

Spring, 1981

Sharp insistent ringing. The alarm? No. Who's
At the door I drift to in a fog,
As my old teacher stumbles in—
Last day of his visit, always the worst.

"I got the papers," he says; plus,
I see, tea, headcheese, some books,
Whatever it took to postpone his hangover
—Watery eyes, sea-blue and uncertain; rolling
Walk like a sailor's (up all night,
I slept in when he went prowling at dawn);
Voice hoarse, and too intent on being understood:

"I've only had a few shandies, for Christ sake.
Don't think I do this all the time at home."

I fill a kettle, take down plates;
As he recites or invents items in the news:

—*Telepathic Twins Separated At Birth;* embarrassing celebrity
Deaths, highjinks of animal mimicry;
JFK Alive In Geneva Hospital; Aphasic Murders Mother
With One Hand As The Other Hand Struggles To Stop Him—

Then more drinks; telephone calls;
More Ramones, Beach Boys, show tunes;
A nap before his long drive home . . .

Day lost in a daze like so many of our days.
Until the next time;

—Until, weeks later, just home from work,
The phone ringing as I enter the apartment:
"I have very bad news—Mark was killed last night."

Mark *killed,* I find myself thinking—

In a bar . . . ? Mugged . . . ? A knife? Gunplay?

Mark? Come on—
This is too *West Side Story.*
Has to be one of his jokes.
"Who are you?
Who put you up to this?"

As *broken steering column   too much wine   stone wall*

Careen past before
Crashing to a stop.

"EVIDENCE"

Believe me it's an awful thing to kibitz on a man
and his wife, and hear what they really talk about.

—August. Cape Cod. Bluffs. Vines,
Grass, a few stunted birches where what's left
Of a cliff rises to divide the ocean
From the parking lot of the Atlantic
Bar & Grille. On the corner of two dead
End streets an exposed "chalet." She watches him
Write a letter: greetings, bus schedule,
Directions. Out of a morning's
Fog their houseguest looms—he and she and he
Share a cottage for a week.

. . . A rattle of leaves overhead.
Three trees hooked by the wind beget an inclining L
For a pair of hammocks—
Jane, restless, chats and swings
As the spare Tarzan stalks a book inside;
Shape we live in,
Shaping the way we live.

Sunset strolls to the adjacent watering hole . . .
LIVE BANDS! Drunk, dead-eyed locals.
Jokey dancing, leading, unsteady talk—
Remarkable, unremarked disappearances.
. . . We sober up in the dark
With loud, reckless swims—on a dare
Who will hazard the most?
One night straining to the warning buoys
That loop the bay in a clanging, iridescent necklace.

she's stronger than she looks   pulling him
out of the backseat while i guide her with a pocket flash
blind triple-turns   no sign   his lights out on vodka
doctored with tuinals   tomorrow's hit and run
G-L-R   G-L-R-R-K already drowning in vomit

Florid and shaky over breakfast . . .
Sleepy jabberings, half-sentences droned
As through a stroke . . . His fingers probe
A rat's nest of uncurling hair,
Yanking, pressing, twisting,
Before exploding in a squall
Of splashy pamphlets and a project—
"Any takers for diving lessons at that marina we passed?"
. . . Her thesis; my . . . hangover;
Waving our hands, shaking our heads,
We sink into the "extra" room,
Scavenge for pleasure . . .
Hooks that tear through flesh
Even as they bind it.

Later, out for a walk with her Nikon,
We stumble on our own project: "Evidence—
The Oblique Account of an Illicit Affair,"
Each photograph like a Dutch Interior
With its own tacit narrative:
My hand gripping her thigh, moving with
The muscle as she stretches for the clutch . . .
An empty, ruined bed,
Three departing shadows . . . And then stumble off again, grinning—
"But who would shoot the pictures?"

helter skelter dead in the middle of relating
a joke about who killed david kennedy i leap
heels over head into the front seat cracking
the steering column and launching the datsun
hell and high water into the grill of an unsuspecting jeep
'JAWS OF LIFE' CAN'T SAVE 3 TANGLED IN FREAK CAPE CRASH

Another night . . . Exhaling concentration,
With both hands she stirs the pot to a boil . . .
Through the water she studies my face,
Then his, as she poles, blending
The contents of a small sack I filled in Chinatown
With the full basket he hauled dripping from the docks;
Black mushrooms, pared pork, water chestnuts stroke
Past baby shrimp and scallops—
Blowing once, twice, to cool
What she's of two minds to swallow
. . . Hot and sour bouillabaisse?
"My wife," he says, rubbing his abdomen.

I linger after they go to bed.
Killing Heinekens; spinning records—
Mixing standards from their traveling collection
With my own deadpan presents: "I Stand Accused,"
"Dark End of the Street," "Getting Mighty Crowded,"
"He'll Have to Go."

it was late, now, and the rain
made the night darker . . . tipsy, i kept tripping
and sliding . . . i didn't know he was there
until he spoke—until a match flared and raised up
to a face beneath a slouch-brimmed hat . . .
that, i said, is a good way of getting killed—
cut the tough guy stuff, he spat back . . . listen,
i've known about you two for a long time . . . don't explain—

things happen that way . . . hey—we fall
into our lives . . . but don't you want to get off
this merry-go-round? . . . yeah, she knows
i'm talking to you . . . look, here are my keys—
catch—why not . . . take a spin someplace . . .

On my way to the bathroom
I stop outside their bedroom door—

In the living room a guitar feeds back,
The hot distorted notes soar and scud
Before they're ripped back into the rhythm—

On the porch bushes scratch at the screen,
Heaving like the sea after a high wind—

Through the window beams from a wandering car
Climb the wall—

A rattle of leaves overhead—

August. Cape Cod. Bluffs. Vines,
Grass, a few stunted birches where what's left. . . .

7

"BACKWARDS AND FORWARDS"

"Passion, it's so much bigger
Than sex; a certain level of anticipation,
Unexplored limits—

And you don't do that with someone you've known 10 years.

It's the music too—live,
When I catch the jolt through the floor—
And I just don't feel I'm here anymore.

But you don't want to be on edge all the time either . . .

This probably won't get any easier—
Passionate encounters tend to become addictive."

                        •

"That Sunday I wasn't sure anything would happen . . .

It was like sitting through a thunder and lightning storm—
Except no rain.

I love your accent—but oh my God,
If we keep talking
We might *like* each other—

And then there wouldn't be loopholes,
Or excuses, or good one-liners . . .

Write me at work—I hate to think this ends
Getting mail from you."

•

"Next week I'm having lunch
With a man I haven't seen in—holy shit, is it 12 years?
I could tell I was making him crazy
Over the phone. We'll see . . .

I never return to the scenes of past crimes.

The idea of a relationship
That's basically a friendship with the odd sexual
Moment thrown in
Is unbelievably appealing to me—

But I've never pulled it off."

•

"Listen. We've got to have a big talk.
I'm hating having to lie all the time—
And I'm starting to make comparisons . . .
It's getting me crazy.

I know that if I told him
He'd make me stop seeing you
—Or go—
And I'm just about certain what I'd do . . .

Listen. I don't like myself this way.
This hurts me too. Listen!"

8

LAST TIMES: NIGHT

Fall, 1979

Stayed away for days;
unable to imagine,
refusing to think about

how easy it should be
to get up, shower, dress
and bus across town

to watch an old man gaining
years by the hour, shrinking,
bottle dripping

nourishment,
machines feeding poisons into swollen
wasted arms,

twisted and rolling as he repeats
rhythmically, dimly,
"God, oh, God,"

to the dropped ceiling;
stuck on the words
the way a falling climber

bites the rope
rock chewed through miles above;
invoking nothing;

just as on his last night, 3 A.M.,
the phone kept ringing and ringing
—could only be

mother, alone at the hospital,
dialing back
as soon as she hangs up

crazy to hear herself say:
"If you want to see your father
die—this is it—he's stopped talking."

9

"CLUBLAND"

> *I hung up . . . That night I did something*
> *I hadn't done in years. I prayed.*

A barrel in the kitchen
Waits to receive the bottle I'm drinking;
At the bottom of the barrel
Other bottles—

> The phone I keep picking up,
> Dialing only to hang up—

Rocking chair, glasses, ears, nose, chin,
Double in the double-pane window;
Doubled again by the Guinness—

> *A leather bar gone to hell—*

Smoke uncoiling in cool ribbons from a semicircle
Of overhead lamps, each white-hot and unblinking; no light-
Show here, only shooting star B.U. girls trailing
Glitter, as they dance,
Flashing studded belts, smiles, and fuck-me shoes
Toward the band that, inches away, twitches and pulses
Over them. Their boyfriends, cast off in groups by the PA,
Gape and drink, flexing spandex or fingering
Chords on the necks of their beers . . . All alone in a corner,
Two slumming models in his-and-her matching
Jackets, haircuts, and eye shadow, tease
A blackened mirror that once unriddled

Ramrods, fist fuckers, and rough trade,
Their fierce codes—keys, insignia, colored
Handkerchiefs—as sly and unequivocal as a Church Father's.

When the first ragged act's history,
The swaggering frontmen, identical twins, wheedle
Drinks from the kids near the stage;
My date, a local music critic, points
At a Siouxsie Sioux lookalike
Parked by the dressing-room door—
"One night the guitar player
Got trashed enough to take her home.
When he was through, he disappeared to take a piss,
But sent his brother back;
Then he screwed her too . . .
She still doesn't know this happened!"

Between sets the show goes on—Lao Tse,
Timeless neighborhood fixture, pushing
80 but boyish in his olive toupee
And leather pants, demonstrates Tai Chi
Before a jar of plastic flowers
He's offering to the next group, his favorite;
My date scampers past with Anton
—Unflappable "manager" of Scurvy the Bat,
He'll play rhythm in the Wild Motel Dwarfs Friday and Saturday,
230 lbs. of game good cheer—
"I'm picking up a press kit, sweetie,
I'll be back in a coupla minutes."

Squirming onto a stool by an idle Ms. Pacman,
I almost elude the middle band:
Icy synth-wizards into random pain . . .
Later, I cruise the aisles,

Shadow a pretty skinhead
Combing out her friend's hair—
"Can you believe all the cute guys here?
I keep wanting to go up to them
And scream, I love you, can I have your baby!"

House lights already up, a breakneck Scurvy
Careers into the final encore
As my date returns with a thick envelope and a cassette—
"Come on, let's go back to my place."

From the window of a 7-11 by the cabstand
The Weekly World News *reassures*
THERE IS SEX AFTER DEATH MEDIUMS SAY.

On my lap through the Back Bay—
"Anton called me a gossip . . . Can you believe it?
The people I tell things to don't tell other people!

. . . Oh Robert . . . I'm so bad . . .
I went back to his house for a tape,
Sorta drunk, so I jumped on his bed—
Then I fucked him . . .
Don't look at me that way,
Like you're going to be sick . . ."

On the floor of her apartment she turns
And licks the last dot of white powder off a record jacket—
"God, I never made it with two people
On the same day before . . .

What are you doing here?

One more beer
And I want to go to sleep . . .

Do you think I should take a valium?

Please stay . . .

Sorry . . . I'm really wasted."

Rocking chair, glasses, ears, nose, chin,
Double in the double-pane window;
Doubled again by the Guinness—

I watch the Guinness bottle spin in the air,
Arc toward one of my faces;
I watch my features duck and blur
When it bounces back into my chest—

                  The phone I keep picking up,
                  Dialing only to hang up—

A barrel in the kitchen
Waits to receive the bottle I'm drinking—

10

LAST TIMES: MORNING

First snow of the year, but late; and
Light, blowing in the empty, sunny street . . .

      Unrelenting sun,
Bearing down through a high, round window,
Hacks out and trims a small stage,
Then pierces the bed like a spotlight;
As last night's impatient forces
—Overdressed, underrehearsed actors
With names like "Desire" and "Necessity"—

Play themselves out.

Her new curls, blonde streaks
And patches, settling as she talks;

Eyes clouding over;
Then wetly brightening;
As they watch him
Watching her do what she says she has to do;

Her "we thought we could save each other":

Head shaking no;
Her long arm cutting through
His *"but can't we still"*—

Until all clears.

The storm's ending; whatever stirs and gusts
Scatters
Over the same rolling, motionless drifts.

—But with nothing else
To do or say;
No audience but themselves:
Once more, for old time's sake?

"We can't—it would be too sad."

                    "I know.
Every minute I'd be thinking, this is the last time."

11

"Dear R——

I know I should have called but for various reasons I have
been feeling tired & feeling a need to see the center of things.

I also haven't changed my mind.

Maybe you're right about some things but now I feel I want
my life to be as smooth & easy as possible.

I want to concentrate on digging deeper alone & not on scat-
tering myself around.

The new career thing seems very important & exciting to me
& needs attention.

I am sorry but I just couldn't face having a conversation about
it all.

I just didn't want to feel I was letting you down.

I am tired of letting people down.

I'm feeling frayed & must just burrow in someplace safe.

For whatever reasons that's the story."

12.

What you've just read, if you've read it,
is the statement.

The story behind the story

        In Weegee's photograph
It's all black and white.
—"Weegee the Famous," prowling Manhattan after
Midnight for the *Daily News,* his studio
A restless Black Maria driven by instinct
And a police radio; his high-speed
Infra-red film—newly developed
For reconnaissance flights—would expose lovers
From the protective gloom of 3D movie houses,
Or on summer nights, shameless, in the sand at Coney Island
—A lone young woman gazes down
From a lifeguard's watchtower, chewing the tips of her fingers . . .

The story behind the story

        In "Victory Celebration 1945"
The furtive, unfair flash locks on
A no-longer young sailor and the dark body of a woman
(Her features swallowed up by his) locking into
A kiss, abrupt and jittery—

Her right hand holding fast to a thick comb,
In his left the still burning end of a war-issue cigarette;

Fingers embroiled in her hair, her other arm is caught
Between them—thrusting him back, or urging

Him in and closer, as his face
Cut by fatigue or dissipation or laughter
Presses her lips, or down into her neck;

Over their shoulders a grinning civilian in a straw hat,
Pleased with the victory, or with himself
Like a deaf-mute in a telephone booth,

As above them a soldier has drifted by—
"At ease," hands firmly in his own
Pockets, legs stiffening
Or about to carry him away—

And turned: Face puffy with desire,
Mouth tight, even; his envy at odds
With the grim sense he's seen them before,
His eyes lock on the celebrating couple—

>   *At the clear center whose edges fade,*
> *Not me looking down at them;*
> *But back into the flash and shadow of our few minutes*
> *Hand in hand down a crowded avenue, oblivious*
> *Of detection, running—;*

Another story   behind the story.